Crash BANG Boom

Exploring Literary Devices through Children's Literature

Karen A. Gibson

UpstartBooks

Fort Atkinson, Wisconsin

Acknowledgments

I would like to thank the teachers of the Pasadena Independent School District for sharing their ideas with me so that I can share them with other teachers.

I owe a debt of gratitude to the following people for cheering me on:

Dr. Lee Mountain who believed in me when I didn't;

My friends and co-workers who are a constant encouragement to me;

My precious family: David, Kelly, Jeremy, Mandy, Mom, Dad and others who understood when I was "too busy."

Published by UpstartBooks
W5527 Highway 106
P.O. Box 800
Fort Atkinson, Wisconsin 53538-0800
1-800-448-4887

© Karen A. Gibson, 2002
Cover design: Wendy Haagensen

The paper used in this publication meets the minimum requirements of American National Standard for Information Science — Permanence of Paper for Printed Library Material. ANSI/NISO Z39.48-1992.

Library of Congress Cataloging-in-Publication Data
Gibson, Karen A., 1952-
  Crash, bang, boom : exploring literary devices through children's
literature / Karen A. Gibson.
      p. cm.
Includes bibliographical references.
  ISBN 1-57950-041-2 (alk. paper)
  1. Children's literature--Study and teaching (Elementary)--United
States. 2. Reading (Elementary)--United States. 3. Children--Books and
reading--United States. I. Title.
  LB1575.5.U5 G53 2002
    372.64--dc21
                                    2002014243

Contents

I See ... You See ...

How Are You Feeling?

Words, Words, Words

Same Sorts of Sounds

Crash! Bang! Boom!

Grouchy as a Bear

Introduction

Educators across the United States are pondering how to motivate their students to read while teaching them the skills they need to pass state reading tests. As more states are administering tests, teachers and library media specialists are searching for ways to teach reading skills that turn their students on to reading.

One of the most promising methods that educators have discovered is using picture books to introduce and reinforce explicit reading skills. Imagine a media specialist surrounded by third graders who are listening intently as she reads *If You Give a Mouse a Cookie* by Laura Joffe Numeroff. As the media specialist reads, she points out the chain of cause and effect relationships demonstrated in this delightful picture book. By doing this, she is teaching a reading skill in a fun and informative manner.

This group of third graders is participating in a reading skills lesson without doing a worksheet or listening to a lecture. They have the events of a story to tie to a reading skill. Later, when asked to identify cause and effect relationships in other stories or in real life situations, they will be able to transfer their knowledge from *If You Give a Mouse a Cookie*.

Many educators agree that practicing reading skills with worksheets alone can turn children off to reading. The worksheets force children to look at print in a meaningless context by drilling them with exercises and paper-and-pencil tests.

Picture books are the perfect genre for teaching reading skills to elementary school students because their length (usually 32 pages) enables them to be read in one sitting, the illustrations keep the interest of the students and their large format makes them easy for all students to see when gathered around the teacher. By following a picture book reading with an activity, the reading skill is emphasized and reinforced in the student's mind.

How to Use This Book

Crash, Bang, Boom provides you with the strategies and lessons that make using picture books both fun and educational for your students. All of the lessons can be done in the classroom or in the media center. The lessons used in the media center might benefit from a follow-up lesson in the classroom.

Each lesson in *Crash, Bang, Boom* includes a summary of the story, an activity that reinforces the skill and a list of the multiple intelligences addressed in the lesson. John Gardner's Theory of Multiple Intelligences suggests that individuals have strengths in certain areas and that they learn better when presented with information using the intelligence they are most comfortable with. In order to reach all children, it is important for educators to address as many intelligences as possible in each lesson.

As an educator, you have access to a gold mine of resources to help students master the literary skills they need to pass your state's assessment. This book contains 55 lessons in teaching literary skills using 55 different picture books. You can use one idea a week and still have some left over!

Happy Reading!

Getting the Big Picture

Titles for Teaching Main Idea

The main idea is the "big idea" that the author is attempting to relay to the reader. It is the underlying meaning of the story. Main idea is sometimes referred to as *theme*. Most of the time, main ideas are implied rather than stated explicitly.

Because each reader brings different life experiences to the reading of a story, main idea is often a difficult skill for students. One student may think that the main idea of *Charlotte's Web* is friendship, while another child may think that Charlotte saving Wilbur is the main idea. Main idea is a skill that needs a lot of classroom discussion time. The following books will help in that discussion.

Books Used in This Chapter

dePaola, Tomie. ***Oliver Button Is a Sissy***. Harcourt, 1979.

Cannon, Janell. ***Verdi***. Harcourt, 1997.

Polacco, Patricia. ***Thank You, Mr. Falker***. Philomel Books, 1998.

Burleigh, Robert. ***Home Run: The Story of Babe Ruth***. Silver Whistle, 1998.

Turner, Priscilla. ***The War Between the Vowels and the Consonants***. Farrar, Straus & Giroux, 1999.

Oliver Button Is a Sissy

Book Summary

Oliver Button doesn't like to do the things that boys usually do. The boys tease him and the girls stick up for him. But Oliver doesn't let the teasing stop him from doing what he loves the best.

Lesson

1. Draw a large star on a transparency or on chart paper.

2. Write "Main Idea" in the middle of the star (be sure to leave enough room to write the main idea underneath).

3. Explain main idea.

4. Read *Oliver Button Is a Sissy* to the students.

5. Write the main idea in the star. It should be similar to: *Oliver Button proves that he is not a sissy but a star.*

6. Brainstorm the ways that Oliver proved he was a star. Write each statement on a point of the star. For example:

   Oliver did not let his classmates' teasing change his desire to act.

   Oliver practiced every day.

Multiple Intelligences Addressed

Verbal/Linguistic Intelligence; Visual/Spatial Intelligence; Intrapersonal Intelligence; Interpersonal Intelligence

Verdi

Book Summary

A young python named Verdi is afraid of growing slow and boring like the older snakes in the jungle.

Lesson

1. Cut sheets of green construction paper into 4″ x 11″ strips. Attach six strips lengthwise. Cut the ends to resemble a snake.

2. Read *Verdi* to the students.

3. Explain main idea to the students. Ask them what the main idea of *Verdi* is. It should be something similar to: *Verdi was afraid of getting old and boring like the other snakes in the forest. But he found as he grew older that each age is special because an individual never changes on the inside.*

4. Write the main idea that the students come up with on the first section of the snake. On each additional section, brainstorm some of the details that added up to the main idea. For example:

   Verdi thought that Umbles and Aggie were boring because they lazed around all day.

   Verdi jumped and played in the forest.

   Verdi was covered in mud and decided not to wash off because he thought being brown and gloppy was better than being green and lazy.

Multiple Intelligences Addressed

Verbal/Linguistic Intelligence; Visual/Spatial Intelligence; Intrapersonal Intelligence; Interpersonal Intelligence

Thank You, Mr. Falker

Book Summary

Trisha is excited about going to school, but she soon discovers that she has difficulty learning to read. Trisha is embarrassed until she meets a very special teacher who helps her overcome her reading problem.

Lesson

1. Explain main idea to the students.

2. Introduce *Thank You, Mr. Falker* and tell the students that the author wrote the book about a real teacher she had in fifth grade.

3. Read *Thank You, Mr. Falker* to the students.

4. Discuss the main idea of the story. It should be something similar to: *Trisha was thankful that her teacher, Mr. Falker, taught her to read.*

Additional Activity

Determine the main idea of specific paragraphs or pages in the story.

Multiple Intelligences Addressed

Verbal/Linguistic Intelligence; Visual/Spatial Intelligence; Intrapersonal Intelligence; Interpersonal Intelligence

Home Run: The Story of Babe Ruth

Book Summary

Home Run: The Story of Babe Ruth is a story of the legendary Babe Ruth as he prepares to hit a home run. The story is supplemented with baseball cards detailing Babe Ruth's career.

Lesson

1. Ask the students to name all of the baseball players they can think of. Write the names on a transparency or on chart paper.

2. Explain that the story you are going to read is about the man many people believe was the greatest baseball player who ever lived. Discuss which player they named might be the subject of the book.

3. Show the students the first picture in the book and ask if they recognize the player. Several students will probably know that this is a picture of Babe Ruth.

4. Read *Home Run: The Story of Babe Ruth* to the students. Do not read the baseball cards yet.

5. Explain main idea to the students. Ask them what the main idea of the story is. It should be similar to: *Babe Ruth was a great baseball player who loved the game and changed baseball forever.*

6. Explain that the baseball cards in the book are the details that support the main idea. Pass the book around and have a different student read each baseball card aloud.

Multiple Intelligences Addressed

Verbal/Linguistic Intelligence; Visual/Spatial Intelligence; Interpersonal Intelligence; Intrapersonal Intelligence

The War Between the Vowels and the Consonants

Book Summary

The vowels and consonants have always been enemies, so no one is surprised when a war breaks out between them. But when the vowels and consonants are confronted with a common enemy, they learn that they must work together in order to survive.

Lesson

1. Put the following groups of letters on a transparency or on chart paper:

   ntrntnl (the word "international" without vowels)

   aio (the word "airport" without consonants)

   Note: You might want to put up additional groups of letters to match the reading level of your students.

2. Ask the students if they can read the nonsense words. Talk about what might be missing from each word. Explain that the story you are going to read might give them a clue about what is missing.

3. Read *The War Between the Vowels and the Consonants* to the students.

4. Ask the students if they know what is missing from the nonsense words. Discuss missing vowels and consonants and see if the students can guess what the words might be. It might be helpful to let them know which vowels or consonants go in the nonsense words.

5. Explain main idea to the students.

6. Ask the students to pick a partner. Have them discuss what they think the main idea of the book is. After a few minutes, discuss the main idea as a class. It should be similar to: *The vowels and consonants learned that they needed to work together in order to win the war.* Write the main idea on the board.

Multiple Intelligences Addressed

Verbal/Linguistic Intelligence; Visual/Spatial Intelligence; Intrapersonal Intelligence; Interpersonal Intelligence

Where? When?

Titles for Teaching Setting

Understanding the setting of a story often determines comprehension of the story. For example, if a student has no background knowledge of the times and places of the Civil War, Patricia Polacco's *Pink and Say* will be much more difficult to understand.

Setting can include location, weather, time period, time of day and passage of time. Some stories contain a great deal of description of the setting while other stories expect the reader to already know the setting. In fairy tales, for example, readers are expected to know that the story took place "long ago and far away."

One good way to teach setting is to read stories where the setting is integral to the story line, then discuss the setting. Another strategy is to take a well-known story and have the students rewrite it using a new setting. For example, you might take the story *The Three Bears* and move them out of the forest and into the White House.

Books Used in This Chapter

Calmenson, Stephanie. ***The Principal's New Clothes***. Scholastic, 1989.

dePaola, Tomie. ***The Legend of the Bluebonnet***. Putnam Publishing Group, 1996.

San Souci, Robert D. ***The Talking Eggs: A Folktale From the American South***. Dial Books for Young Readers, 1989.

Lowell, Susan. ***Cindy Ellen: A Wild Western Cinderella***. HarperCollins, 2000.

Kellogg, Steven. ***Johnny Appleseed: A Tall Tale***. Morrow Junior Books, 1988.

The Principal's New Clothes

Book Summary

In this modern version of *The Emperor's New Clothes*, the principal of P.S. 88 is outsmarted by two unscrupulous tailors. The tailors tell the principal that they will make him a wonderful suit that only intelligent people who are good at their jobs will be able to see.

Lesson

1. Read *The Emperor's New Clothes* by Hans Christian Anderson (Abbeville Press, Inc., 2001) to the students.

2. Explain setting.

3. Ask the students what the setting was for *The Emperor's New Clothes*. Explain that the author of *The Principal's New Clothes* took *The Emperor's New Clothes* and changed the setting.

4. Read *The Principal's New Clothes* to the students.

5. Ask students what the new setting of the story is. Discuss how the change of setting changed the story.

Additional Activity

Divide students into groups of five or six. Assign each group a setting and ask them to develop a skit that changes *The Principal's New Clothes* and *The Emperor's New Clothes* to an entirely new setting. Possible settings include: doctor's office, airplane factory, the White House, etc.

Multiple Intelligences Addressed

Verbal/Linguistic Intelligence; Visual/Spatial Intelligence; Body/Kinesthetic Intelligence; Intrapersonal Intelligence; Interpersonal Intelligence

The Legend of the Bluebonnet

Book Summary

The Legend of the Bluebonnet is a retelling of the Comanche Indian legend about a little girl's sacrifice and how it brought the bluebonnet flower to Texas.

Lesson

1. Explain setting to the students.

2. Ask the students to listen carefully as you read the story. They should try to remember any words that might be clues to the setting (they may write them down if necessary). Explain that you will discuss the words at the end of the story.

3. Read *The Legend of the Bluebonnet* to the students.

4. Make a transparency of the chart on page 16. Record the words that the students remember on the chart. Possibilities include:

   Character names: She-Who-Is-Alone

   Place names: tipis

   Other words: leggings

5. When you have recorded all of the words that you remember, read the story again and write down any other words you find.

Multiple Intelligences Addressed

Verbal/Linguistic Intelligence; Visual/Spatial Intelligence; Interpersonal Intelligence

Words That Give Clues to the Setting

Write down all of the words that give clues about the setting of *The Legend of the Bluebonnet*.

Character Names	Place Names	Other Words

The Talking Eggs: A Folktale from the American South

Book Summary

In *The Talking Eggs: A Folktale From the American South*, Blanche, the kind younger sister, follows all of an old woman's directions and is rewarded with great riches, but Blanche's sister Rose makes fun of the old woman and is duly rewarded.

Lesson

1. Read *The Talking Eggs: A Folktale From the American South* to the students.

2. Explain setting. Discuss the setting of the story by asking the following questions:

   Where did the story take place? How do you know?

   When did the story take place? What clues told you so?

3. Use the picture and word clues to determine the setting. Picture clues that indicate that the story took place long ago are: the style of clothing worn by the characters, the horse and buggy for transportation and the well where the characters went to draw their water. The chickens and cows indicate that the setting of the story is on a farm. Word clues are: "lived on a farm" (farm), "raised a few chickens, some beans, and a little cotton" (farm), "go milk my cow" (farm), "ran away into the woods" (woods), "back in the old days" (long ago).

4. Choose three or four students to color the swampy setting on a large sheet of butcher paper.

5. On separate sheets of paper, have the rest of the students draw some of the fantastic objects that appeared in the story, i.e., the talking eggs, the cows with the curly horns, the colorful chickens, the jeweled eggs, etc.

6. Cut the pictures out and glue them to the butcher paper so you have a mural of *The Talking Eggs: A Folktale From the American South*. Display the mural for everyone to enjoy.

Multiple Intelligences Addressed

Verbal/Linguistic Intelligence; Visual/Spatial Intelligence; Interpersonal Intelligence; Body/Kinesthetic Intelligence

Cindy Ellen: A Wild Western Cinderella

Book Summary

In this wild western retelling of *Cinderella*, Cindy Ellen loses one of her diamond spurs at a square dance.

Lesson

1. Read *Cinderella* by Charles Perrault (Simon & Schuster Children's Books, 1997) to the students.

2. Explain setting.

3. Explain that the author of *Cindy Ellen: A Wild Western Cinderella* took *Cinderella* and changed the setting. Have the students listen carefully for any setting clues in the story. They should also look for clues in the illustrations.

4. Read *Cindy Ellen: A Wild Western Cinderella* to the students.

5. Make a transparency of the chart on page 19. Compare the settings of *Cindy Ellen: A Wild Western Cinderella* and *Cinderella*. Clues include:

   Cinderella: people are wearing old-fashioned clothes, Princess

   Cindy Ellen: ranches, horses

Multiple Intelligences Addressed

Verbal/Linguistic Intelligence; Visual/Spatial Intelligence; Interpersonal Intelligence

Compare the Settings

Write down all of the word and picture clues from *Cinderella* and *Cindy Ellen: A Wild Western Cinderella* that help you figure out each story's setting.

Cinderella	Cindy Ellen
Setting: long ago in a place where there were kings and queens	**Setting:** the Wild West

Johnny Appleseed: A Tall Tale

Book Summary

Johnny Appleseed: A Tall Tale presents the life of John Chapman (Johnny Appleseed). It describes his love of nature, his kindness to animals and his physical fortitude.

Lesson

1. Explain setting to the students.

2. Ask the students to listen to all of the places that Johnny Appleseed traveled during his lifetime. These places are the setting of the story.

3. Read *Johnny Appleseed: A Tall Tale* to the students.

4. Use a map of the United States to trace the story of Johnny's life. Place small flags or apple-shaped paper on each of the places Johnny visited.

Multiple Intelligences Addressed

Verbal/Linguistic Intelligence; Visual/Spatial Intelligence; Interpersonal Intelligence; Body/Kinesthetic Intelligence

It Happened Because ...

Titles for Teaching Cause and Effect

Cause and effect is a skill that students will be called on to recognize in real life situations. "If you fight with your sister, you will be sent to your room." "If you don't study for the spelling test, you will get a bad grade." An excellent way to help students realize that their actions cause certain effects to take place is to point out cause and effect relationships in literature.

In order to recognize a cause and effect relationship in a book, students must be aware that certain things happen because of other events or actions. It is important for students to realize that the cause always happens first and the effect follows. This can be confusing to students because sometimes the cause follows the effect in a statement. An example is, "We didn't go to the picnic because it rained." *It rained* is the cause and *we didn't go to the picnic* is the effect. Students need a great deal of practice before they understand cause and effect relationships. The following books will help.

Books Used in This Chapter

Numeroff, Laura Joffe. ***If You Give a Pig a Pancake***. HarperCollins, 1999.

Walton, Rick. ***That's What You Get!*** Gibbs Smith, 2000.

Barrett, Judi. ***Cloudy With a Chance of Meatballs***. Aladdin Paperbacks, 1982.

Noble, Trinka Hakes. ***The Day Jimmy's Boa Ate the Wash***. Dial Books for Young Readers, 1984.

Shannon, David. ***The Rain Came Down***. Blue Sky Press, 2000.

If You Give a Pig a Pancake

Book Summary

When a small girl gives a pig a pancake, she finds that one thing always leads to another.

Lesson

1. Explain cause and effect relationships.

2. Read *If You Give a Pig a Pancake* to the students. Talk about the causes and effects in the story.

3. Have a Cause and Effect Game Show. You will need two front desk bells (available at office supply stores).

4. Divide the class into two teams. One student from each team stands at the front of the room with the bells on a table in front of him or her.

5. Read one of the cause and effect statements on page 23. When one of the students recognizes the cause in the sentence, he or she should ring the bell. If the student states the correct cause, his or her team gets a point and the student keeps playing. The other student must return to his or her desk. If the student is incorrect, the other student has a chance to answer and earn a point.

6. The game continues until one team reaches a predetermined number of points or until every student has had a chance to play.

Additional Activity

Read the other books by Laura Joffe Numeroff (*If You Give a Mouse a Cookie, If You Give a Moose a Muffin, If You Take a Mouse to the Movies* and *If You Take a Mouse to School*) and have students come up with the cause and effect statements. Play the Cause and Effect Game Show.

Multiple Intelligences Addressed

Verbal/Linguistic Intelligence; Visual/Spatial Intelligence; Interpersonal Intelligence; Body/Kinesthetic Intelligence

Find the Cause

Sentences for the Cause and Effect Game Show from the *If You Give a Pig a Pancake* Lesson on page 22. The **bolded text** indicates the cause.

1. The girl gave the pig some syrup **because the pig liked it on her pancake.**

2. **As a result of eating syrup,** the pig got sticky.

3. **The pig got sticky,** so she wanted to take a bath.

4. **Because the girl gave the pig bubbles in her bath,** the pig will need a toy to play with.

5. The pig will get homesick **because the girl gave the pig a rubber duck which reminded the pig of her life on the farm.**

6. **The girl played the piano for the pig.** As a result, the pig started dancing.

7. **Because the pig wants the girl to take a picture of her,** the girl will have to look for her camera.

8. **The pig has written letters to all her friends,** so the girl will have to take the pig to the mailbox.

9. **Because the pig sees a tree,** she wants to build a tree house.

10. The pig will ask for some more maple syrup, **because she got sticky from hanging wallpaper.**

That's What You Get!

Book Summary

When a boy gets into all kinds of predicaments, his zany mother explains why the strange things are happening to him.

Lesson

1. Ask the students if they have ever told their parents something and had their parents say, "That's what you get for _____."

2. Explain that this is a cause and effect relationship.

3. Explain that you are going to read a story about a boy who gets into all kinds of crazy and embarrassing situations. When he tells his mother about them, she says, "That's what you get for _____ ," just like their parents did. Of course the difference is that this mother's answers are zany and always rhyme!

4. Begin reading *That's What You Get!* to the students.

5. After you have read several scenarios, allow students to predict what the mother will come up with as a cause for her son's next predicament.

6. Continue reading in this manner until you finish the book.

Multiple Intelligences Addressed

Verbal/Linguistic Intelligence; Visual/Spatial Intelligence; Interpersonal Intelligence; Intrapersonal Intelligence

Cloudy With a Chance of Meatballs

Book Summary

In the town of Chewandswallow all of the food for the inhabitants falls from the sky. Rain falls in the form of soup and juice. It snows mashed potatoes and green peas. Sometimes the wind even blows in hamburgers. All is wonderful until the weather takes a turn for the worse.

Lesson

1. Cut five cloud shapes out of white construction paper. On each cloud write the following cause and effect signal words: *because, so, since, therefore* and *as a result of.*

2. Write each cause and effect sentence from page 26 on a strip of paper.

3. Read *Cloudy With a Chance of Meatballs* to the students.

4. Review the meaning of cause and effect relationships.

5. Hand the cloud shapes out to five different students. Hand the first pair of cause and effect sentences out to different students.

6. The cloud students decide how to use their word to indicate cause and effect between the sentences. The cloud students can position the sentence students any way they wish in order to make correct cause and effect statements. For example, using sentence pair 1, the students could create the following possibilities:

    The family realized that a pancake had landed on Henry's face, *so* the family laughed.

    Because the family realized that a pancake had landed on Henry's face, the family laughed.

    The family laughed *because* the family realized that a pancake had landed on Henry's face.

    The family realized that a pancake had landed on Henry's face. *As a result*, the family laughed.

    The family realized that a pancake had landed on Henry's face. *Therefore*, the family laughed.

    Since the family realized that a pancake had landed on Henry's face, the family laughed.

7. Continue with the rest of the cause and effect sentences.

Multiple Intelligences Addressed

Verbal/Linguistic Intelligence; Visual/Spatial Intelligence; Interpersonal Intelligence; Logical/Mathematical Intelligence; Body/Kinesthetic Intelligence

Cause and Effect Sentences

Write each sentence on a strip of paper. Use with the *Cloudy with a Chance of Meatballs* Lesson on page 25.

Cause	Effect
1. The family realized that a pancake had landed on Henry's face.	1. The family laughed.
2. There were no food stores in Chewandswallow.	2. The sky supplied all the food the townspeople wanted.
3. The people watched the weather report on television in the morning.	3. They knew what their meals would be for the day.
4. The townspeople carried plates, cups, glasses, forks, spoons and knives when they went outside.	4. They were prepared for any kind of weather.
5. Sometimes there were leftovers.	5. The townspeople took them home to put in the refrigerator in case they got hungry between meals.
6. Some of the leftover food was emptied in the oceans.	6. The fish, turtles and whales ate it.
7. The food was getting larger and larger.	7. The people were getting frightened.
8. There was a hurricane of bread, rolls and toast.	8. Everyone had to stay indoors.
9. No one could get the huge pancake off of the school.	9. It weighed too much.
10. Everyone ate themselves sick with cream cheese and jelly sandwiches.	10. The day ended with a stomachache.
11. There was a salt and pepper wind.	11. People were sneezing themselves silly.
12. The Sanitation Department gave up trying to clean up the food.	12. The job was too big.
13. Everyone feared for their lives.	13. A decision was made to abandon the town of Chewandswallow.
14. The bread boats held up well.	14. The people built temporary houses out of them.
15. Nobody dared go back to Chewandswallow.	15. They were too afraid.
16. The children ate breakfast faster than usual.	16. They wanted to go sledding with Grandpa.

The Day Jimmy's Boa Ate the Wash

Book Summary

The class trip to the farm is boring until chaos takes over and one zany incident leads to another, even zanier one. But Jimmy's boa constrictor takes the cake when it scares the farmer's wife.

Lesson

1. Use the pattern on page 28 to cut out 10 t-shirt shapes from two different colors of paper. Write the causes from page 28 on one color of t-shirt. Write the effects from page 28 on the other color of t-shirt. Clothespin all of the cause t-shirts to a clothesline stretched across the media center.

2. Read *The Day Jimmy's Boa Ate the Wash* to the students.

3. Discuss cause and effect.

4. Ask the students to listen carefully to all of the cause and effect relationships as you read the story again.

5. On a transparency or chart paper, write down all of the cause and effect relationships that the students remember.

6. Give one effect t-shirt to each student and ask them to clothespin it to the corresponding cause t-shirt.

Multiple Intelligences Addressed

Verbal/Linguistic Intelligence; Visual/Spatial Intelligence; Interpersonal Intelligence; Body/Kinesthetic Intelligence

Cause and Effect T-Shirts

Enlarge the t-shirt pattern on a photocopier. Make 10 photocopies on two different colors of paper. Write the cause sentences on one color of t-shirt and the effect sentences on the other color of t-shirt. Cut the t-shirts out. Use with *The Day Jimmy's Boa Ate the Wash* Lesson on page 27.

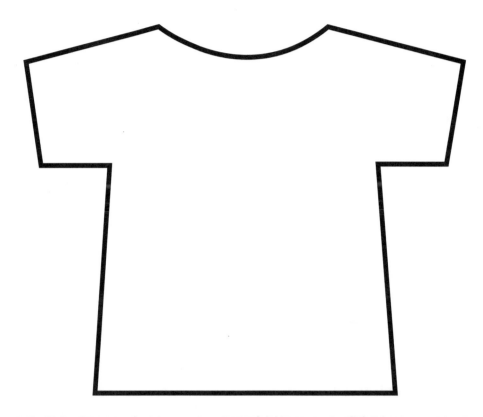

Cause	Effect
The haystack fell on the cow.	The cow cried.
The farmer crashed into the haystack with his tractor.	The haystack fell on the cow.
The farmer yelled at the pigs.	The farmer crashed into the haystack.
The students threw the pigs' corn at each other so the pigs didn't have anything to eat.	The pigs ate the students' lunches.
The students ran out of eggs.	The students threw the pigs' corn.
A boa constrictor got loose in the hen house.	The chickens squawked and flew around.
The hens got excited.	A hen laid an egg.
The egg broke on Jenny's head.	Jenny got mad.
Tommy ducked.	An egg hit Marianne in the face.
A boa constrictor got tangled up in the wash.	The farmer's wife screamed.

The Rain Came Down

Book Summary

When the sky clouds over on a beautiful sunny day, the townspeople and animals get cranky. Each new event causes a chain reaction, until the day comes full circle.

Lesson

1. Read *The Rain Came Down* to the students.

2. Explain cause and effect relationships.

3. Read the book again and ask the students to come up with as many cause and effect relationships as possible. For example:

   The rain came down, so the chickens squawked.
   Because the chickens were squawking, the cats yowled at them.

4. Play a cause and effect game. The object is to get the students to recognize the cause and effect as quickly as possible.

5. Write each cause and effect statement on an index card. Drop the cards into a box.

6. Divide the students into pairs. Have each pair select a card from the box.

7. Each pair presents their cause and effect scenario to the class. They must present it without using words or sounds, as in Charades. Give the students a few minutes to prepare their presentation.

8. Time each presentation to see how long it takes for the class to guess the cause and effect relationship.

Multiple Intelligences Addressed

Verbal/Linguistic Intelligence; Visual/Spatial Intelligence; Interpersonal Intelligence; Body/Kinesthetic Intelligence

What Happens Next?

Titles for Teaching Prediction

Predictions are educated guesses about what will happen next in a story. Readers can use the text, titles and illustrations to predict what will most likely or probably occur next. These predictions are only educated guesses. As readers continue reading, they will either confirm, abandon or change their predictions.

Poor readers rarely predict, either correctly or incorrectly. Often they just call out words without anticipating what will happen next. Teachers should let students know that prediction is a necessary skill that does not always have to be "correct" in order to be valuable to the reader. Encouraging your students to improve their prediction skills will help them become better readers.

Books Used in This Chapter

Taback, Simms. *Joseph Had a Little Overcoat*. Viking, 1999.

McNaughton, Colin. *Suddenly*. Harcourt, 1998.

Spinelli, Eileen. *Somebody Loves You, Mr. Hatch*. Simon & Schuster, 1991.

Peet, Bill. *Chester the Worldly Pig*. Houghton Mifflin, 1993.

Van Allsburg, Chris. *Just a Dream*. Houghton Mifflin, 1990.

Joseph Had a Little Overcoat

Book Summary

In this Caldecott Medal book, an overcoat is recycled over and over again into many new garments. The story ends with the moral "You can always make something out of nothing." This book is perfect for teaching prediction because each time Joseph makes something new out of his overcoat, a die-cut hole in the page invites students to predict what the next piece of clothing will be.

Lesson

1. Explain prediction.

2. Read *Joseph Had a Little Overcoat* to the students. Each time you come to a die-cut page, ask the students to predict the next piece of clothing that Joseph will make.

3. Read the story again without showing the illustrations.

4. Ask the students which reading they enjoyed the most, the one where they got to view the illustrations or the one where they didn't see any pictures. Help them see that looking at the pictures helped them make predictions about the story.

Multiple Intelligences Addressed

Verbal/Linguistic Intelligence; Visual/Spatial Intelligence; Interpersonal Intelligence; Intrapersonal Intelligence

Suddenly

Book Summary

Preston Pig is walking home when "suddenly" many things happen to him and to the wicked wolf who is following him.

Lesson

1. Show the students the cover of *Suddenly.* Point out that there are two main characters in the story, the pig and the wolf.

2. Ask the students to predict what is going to happen in the story using the cover illustration as a clue.

3. Begin reading *Suddenly* to the students. Stop each time you read the word "suddenly." Ask the students to predict what they think will happen next. The students will soon discover that they are making two predictions each time. One prediction will concern Preston Pig and the other prediction will be about the wolf. Since the story has a surprise ending, the students will probably make incorrect predictions. Explain that good readers often make incorrect predictions, but as they continue to read, they revise their predictions to fit with the story.

Multiple Intelligences Addressed

Verbal/Linguistic Intelligence; Visual/Spatial Intelligence; Interpersonal Intelligence

Somebody Loves You, Mr. Hatch

Book Summary

An anonymous box of Valentine chocolates turns unhappy Mr. Hatch into a happy neighbor and friend. Then the postman discovers that he has delivered the Valentine candy to the wrong address.

Lesson

1. Explain prediction to the students.

2. Read *Somebody Loves You, Mr. Hatch* until Mr. Goober comes to Mr. Hatch's house.

3. Make a transparency of the chart on page 34. Have the students predict what they think will happen next. Be sure that they use the story to justify their predictions.

4. Continue reading *Somebody Loves You, Mr. Hatch* until Mr. Goober announces that he has an idea.

5. Check off any of the previous predictions that were correct. Explain to the students that skilled readers are constantly making and changing predictions as they read.

6. Once again, have students make predictions for the rest of the book. Finish the story, then discuss the students' predictions.

Multiple Intelligences Addressed

Verbal/Linguistic Intelligence; Visual/Spatial Intelligence; Interpersonal Intelligence; Intrapersonal Intelligence; Logical/Mathematical Intelligence

Class Prediction Worksheet

Predict what you think will happen next in *Somebody Loves You, Mr. Hatch*.

We predict ...	Reasons for our predictions ...

Chester the Worldly Pig

Book Summary

Chester the pig dreams of being a famous circus star. When he finally reaches his goal, he finds that being in the circus is not as exciting as he thought it would be. His escape puts him in the path of danger and excitement and a surprise ending gives him the fame he always dreamed about.

Lesson

1. Explain prediction to the students.

2. Show the students the cover of *Chester the Worldly Pig* and all of the illustrations except the last three pages.

3. Have the students find a partner and discuss what they think the story is going to be about. Ask the students to share their predictions with the group.

4. Read *Chester the Worldly Pig* to the students.

5. Pause after reading the following pages and ask the questions below or choose questions of your own.

   Page 3: How do you think Chester will accomplish his goal of becoming a circus star?

   Page 17: What part do you think Chester will play in the circus?

   Page 25: When Chester escapes from Rosco the clown, what will happen to him next?

   Page 27: What will happen to Chester as he runs away from the bear?

   Page 33: How will Chester escape from the three tramps?

   Page 43: Why do you think the man from the carnival is so excited about buying Chester that he is willing to pay twice what Chester is worth?

6. When you finish the story, ask the students if they guessed that Chester had a map of the world on his hide.

Multiple Intelligences Addressed

Verbal/Linguistic Intelligence; Visual/Spatial Intelligence; Interpersonal Intelligence

Just a Dream

Book Summary

When Walter has a nightmare about a future Earth ruined by pollution, he recognizes the need to take care of the environment.

Lesson

1. Explain prediction to the students.

2. Read *Just a Dream* until Walter goes to sleep. Use some of the questions listed below to ask students to predict what will happen next.

   What will Walter probably see next?

   What do you think will probably happen?

   When Walter goes to the future, he will probably …

   According to the author, it is likely that in the future …

   Based on the picture, Walter will probably …

   What does the author give you reason to believe about the future?

   After reading this page, you can conclude that …

3. At each change of setting, there is a small picture that is perfect for predicting where Walter will visit next. After reading each section, show students the pictures. Discuss what will happen next.

Multiple Intelligences Addressed

Verbal/Linguistic Intelligence; Visual/Spatial Intelligence; Interpersonal Intelligence; Naturalistic Intelligence

I Think ...

Titles for Teaching Inference and Drawing Conclusions

Making inferences and drawing conclusions is the process of looking beyond the written text and judging, deriving, concluding and reasoning. This skill involves using information from the text along with prior knowledge and personal experience to construct meaning.

Even though very young students use inferencing to supply information not given in the text, they do this subconsciously. They need a teacher to explain that the skill will help them improve as readers.

A good way to introduce students to inference is to read them a short passage that you have written about your school, leaving out any visual description. Ask students to explain the pictures they saw in their head when you were reading. Tell the students that people who had never been to your school and had no background knowledge of your school would not have been able to infer the same mental images.

Books Used in This Chapter

Gray, Libba Moore. *Miss Tizzy*. Aladdin Paperbacks, 1998.

Coles, Robert. *The Story of Ruby Bridges*. Scholastic, 1995.

dePaola, Tomie. *The Art Lesson*. Putnam Publishing Group, 1997.

Fox, Mem. *Tough Boris*. Harcourt, 1998.

Raschka, Christopher. *Yo! Yes?* Orchard Books, 1998.

Miss Tizzy

Book Summary

Miss Tizzy is a wonderful friend to all of the children in the neighborhood. She leads them in many exciting activities, but she needs their help when she gets sick.

Lesson

1. Read *Miss Tizzy* to the students. Make sure they chime in on the phrase "and the children loved it."

2. Continue reading until Miss Tizzy gets sick. The story says that the children miss their friend and have an idea. Ask students to predict what the children's idea might be.

3. Discuss the predictions, then read the next page. It says that on Monday the children baked cookies and on Tuesday they put on a puppet show for Miss Tizzy. The students should be able to infer that the children are doing the same things that Miss Tizzy did with them during the week.

4. Have the students predict what will happen on Wednesday, Thursday, Friday and Saturday. Explain inferences to the students. Explain that they were able to make predictions because they inferred things from the story.

Multiple Intelligences Addressed

Verbal/Linguistic Intelligence; Visual/Spatial Intelligence; Interpersonal Intelligence; Musical/Rhythmic Intelligence; Intrapersonal Intelligence

The Story of Ruby Bridges

Book Summary

The Story of Ruby Bridges is the true story of how a six-year-old girl's courage enabled her to be the first African American student to integrate schools in New Orleans.

Lesson

1. Explain the background of *The Story of Ruby Bridges.* Many years ago, black children and white children were not allowed to attend the same schools. A little girl named Ruby Bridges was the first student to attend an all-white elementary school in New Orleans.

2. Explain inferences to the students.

3. Make a transparency of the chart on page 40.

4. Show the students each illustration from the book, one page at a time. As they look at the illustrations, fill in the chart together. Write down what you think the characters are feeling, along with the clues from the illustrations, and what you think the characters are doing, along with the clues from the illustrations. Explain that they are making inferences.

5. Read *The Story of Ruby Bridges* to the students.

6. Discuss the inferences on the chart and whether or not they were correct.

Multiple Intelligences Addressed

Verbal/Linguistic Intelligence; Visual/Spatial Intelligence; Interpersonal Intelligence; Intrapersonal Intelligence

Making Inferences

Use the illustrations from *The Story of Ruby Bridges* to make inferences about what the characters are feeling and doing. Write down the clues from the illustrations that helped you make the inferences.

Picture	Feeling	Clues	Action	Clues
Cover				
Title Page				
Illustration 1				
Illustration 2				
Illustration 3				
Illustration 4				
Illustration 5				
Illustration 6				
Illustration 7				
Illustration 8				
Illustration 9				
Illustration 10				
Illustration 11				
Illustration 12				

The Art Lesson

Book Summary

Tommy is excited about art lessons until he finds out that they are much more regimented than drawing at home—he only gets one piece of paper, has to use school crayons and must copy what the art teacher draws.

Lesson

1. Read *The Art Lesson* to the students.

2. Explain inference. Ask the students to make an inference about who the main character of the story is. Students should be able to infer that the main character is the author himself, Tomie dePaola.

3. Discuss what clues in the story helped the students make this inference.

4. Explain that *The Art Lesson* is an autobiographical book. Share other books written and illustrated by dePaola, such as *Nana Upstairs and Nana Downstairs*, *26 Fairmount Avenue*, *The Baby Sister* and *Here We All Are*. Discuss what other inferences they can draw about the author's life from the other books he has written.

Multiple Intelligences Addressed

Verbal/Linguistic Intelligence; Visual/Spatial Intelligence; Interpersonal Intelligence

Tough Boris

Book Summary

Boris von der Borch is a tough, greedy, fearless pirate who shows a different side when his parrot dies.

Lesson

1. Read *Tough Boris* to the students until just before Boris's parrot dies. (Do not let the students know that the parrot dies.)

2. Use a transparency or chart paper to list all of Boris's characteristics. For example, tough, massive, scruffy, greedy, fearless and scary. Ask the students to draw a conclusion about the type of person that Boris is.

3. Read the rest of the book. Again ask the students to draw a conclusion about Boris and how he felt about his pet parrot.

4. On the final page of the book, show the students the illustration of the little boy who narrated the story. Have the students draw conclusions about the end of the story.

Multiple Intelligences Addressed

Verbal/Linguistic Intelligence; Visual/Spatial Intelligence; Interpersonal Intelligence; Intrapersonal Intelligence

Yo! Yes?

Book Summary

Two lonely boys, one white and one black, meet on a street and become friends. They use almost no dialogue to express themselves, but the reader can infer from the illustrations and the few words that are spoken that the boys form a friendship.

Lesson

1. Explain inferences.

2. Read *Yo! Yes?* to the students.

3. Discuss all of the possible things that could be happening in the book. Accept any plausible explanation as long as the students explain their conclusions with clues from the book. For example, "I can draw the conclusion that the black child is trying to make friends with the white child. My clue from the book was that the black boy was the first to speak and attract the white boy's attention."

4. Discuss which inference seems most likely to be true.

5. Have two students dramatize the action using the dialogue in the book.
   Note: You might want to write each character's dialogue on index cards.

Multiple Intelligences Addressed

Verbal/Linguistic Intelligence; Visual/Spatial Intelligence; Interpersonal Intelligence; Body/Kinesthetic Intelligence; Musical/Rhythmic Intelligence

I See ... You See ...

Titles for Teaching Point of View

Stories are written from a specific viewpoint, often referred to as point of view. It is helpful in the understanding of a story to know whose viewpoint the story is written from. Point of view can refer to the place from which a person views an object or situation. It can also refer to a particular attitude or filter through which someone perceives a situation. Readers should watch for words that clue them in to what an author or character is thinking or feeling.

When students are in junior high and high school, they will be taught the formal points of view—first-person, omniscient, limited omniscient and objective. But younger students can also be introduced to point of view. One strategy is to look at multiple versions of a fairy tale and determine who is telling the story. When that person is determined, that is the point of view from which the story is written. Another method is to have students rewrite a well-known story from a different character's viewpoint. An example might be for students to write *Cinderella* from Prince Charming's point of view.

Books Used in This Chapter

Woodson, Jacqueline. ***The Other Side***. Putnam, 2001.

Rogers, Kenny, and Don Schlitz. ***The Greatest***. Addax Publishing Group, 2000.

Howe, James. ***I Wish I Were a Butterfly***. Harcourt, 1987.

Browne, Anthony. ***Voices In the Park***. DK Publishing, 1998.

Banyai, Istvan. ***Zoom***. Viking Penguin, 1995.

The Other Side

Book Summary

Two little girls, one white and one black, live on either side of a fence that divides their town racially. As they sit on the fence and get to know each other, they become friends.

Lesson

1. Show students the cover of *The Other Side.* Ask the students to predict which girl they think will tell this story. Ask them for the rationale behind their predictions.

2. Explain point of view to the students. Explain that each girl in the story has her own point of view, but this story only tells one girl's point of view.

3. Read *The Other Side* to the students.

4. Discuss how the story would be different if it was told from Annie's point of view.

Multiple Intelligences Addressed

Verbal/Linguistic Intelligence; Visual/Spatial Intelligence; Interpersonal Intelligence; Intrapersonal Intelligence

The Greatest

Book Summary

In *The Greatest*, a young baseball player learns that there is more than one way to be a winner.

Lesson

1. As students enter the room, play the accompanying CD of Kenny Rogers singing "The Greatest."

2. Read *The Greatest* to the students.

3. Ask the students to think about a time when they did not feel good about themselves.

4. Explain how the boy could have been discouraged each time he missed hitting the ball, but that he looked at the situation from a positive point of view. He chose to focus on what a great baseball pitcher he was.

5. Explain point of view to the students. Discuss how point of view can change people's attitudes about a situation.

Multiple Intelligences Addressed

Verbal/Linguistic Intelligence; Visual/Spatial Intelligence; Interpersonal Intelligence; Intrapersonal Intelligence; Musical/Rhythmic Intelligence

I Wish I Were a Butterfly

Book Summary

A wise old spider helps a young cricket realize that everyone is special in their own unique way.

Lesson

1. Give each student a paper butterfly cutout or an illustration of a butterfly. Ask the students to write the following on their butterfly:

   "I wish I were _____ ."

2. Read *I Wish I Were A Butterfly* to the students.

3. After the story, ask the following questions:

   Who did the cricket want to be like?

   What characteristics did the butterfly have that the cricket wished for?

   Who did the butterfly want to be like?

   What characteristics did the cricket have that the butterfly wished for?

4. Explain point of view to the students. Explain that both the cricket and the butterfly were looking at the situation from their own point of view.

5. Explain to the students that everything and everyone is special in their own way.

6. Pass out a paper cricket cutout or an illustration of a cricket. Ask the students to write the following on their cricket:

   "I am special because_____ ."

Multiple Intelligences Addressed

Verbal/Linguistic Intelligence; Visual/Spatial Intelligence; Interpersonal Intelligence; Intrapersonal Intelligence

Voices In the Park

Book Summary

Four characters—a bossy woman, a sad man, a lonely boy and a young girl—enter the same park. Through their eyes, the reader sees four different versions of the same scene.

Lesson

1. On a transparency or chart paper, write: "Bossy Woman," "Sad Man," "Lonely Boy" and "Young Girl."

2. Explain to the students that this book is written in four different voices from four different points of view. Explain point of view to the students.

3. Read each section without showing illustrations. Have the students decide which character told that section of the story.

4. Place the appropriate character in a chart like the one below.

Voice 1	Voice 2	Voice 3	Voice 4

5. Read all four sections in the same manner.

6. Once the students have determined which character goes with which section, read the story again and show the illustrations. Allow students to change their minds if necessary.

Multiple Intelligences Addressed

Verbal/Linguistic Intelligence; Visual/Spatial Intelligence; Interpersonal Intelligence; Body/Kinesthetic Intelligence

Zoom

Book Summary

This picture book presents a series of scenes, each one from farther away and from a different point of view. For example, one of the scenes shows a cowboy watching television in the desert. When seen from a distance, this scene is actually a U.S. postage stamp. The postage stamp is on a letter being held by someone in another part of the world. With each turn of the page, the reader's point of view changes.

Lesson

1. Show the students a camera with a zoom lens. Explain that in order to see a scene up close, you must "zoom in." To see a scene from a distance, you must "zoom out." Explain point of view.

2. Show the students the cover of *Zoom* and ask them to predict what they think the book will be about. Tell them that this is an unusual book, because it has no words. The pictures tell the story.

3. Show students each page of *Zoom*. Allow time for them to realize that each turn of the page zooms out to a larger view of the world. Explain that each picture is seen from a different point of view.

4. Discuss each page and its point of view. Leave the book out so the students can look at it over and over again.

Additional Activity

Have students write a narrative using one of the pictures as a prompt. The pictures with people in them should be written from that person's point of view.

Istvan Banyai's second book, *Re-Zoom* (1995), can be used with this lesson as well.

Multiple Intelligences Addressed

Verbal/Linguistic Intelligence; Visual/Spatial Intelligence; Interpersonal Intelligence; Intrapersonal Intelligence; Logical/Mathematical Intelligence

How Are You Feeling?

Titles for Teaching Characterization

Characters are the most important part of a story because the action usually revolves around one character or a group of characters. Characterization involves everything that the author uses to make readers understand a character better. Characters are developed through appearance, action, dialogue and monologue. An author often describes a character's feelings to allow the reader insight into the character's actions. Because characters' feelings are often inferred, books that directly address how a character feels help students begin to recognize this important literary element.

Teachers can introduce characterization to students by explaining that each student is the main character in his or her own life story. What he does and how she feels makes each person's story unique.

Books Used in This Chapter

Emberley, Ed, and Anne Miranda. **Glad Monster, Sad Monster: A Book About Feelings**. Little, Brown & Company, 1997.

Kachenmeister, Cherryl. **On Monday When It Rained**. Houghton Mifflin, 1996.

Freymann, Saxton, and Joost Elffers. **How Are You Peeling? Foods with Moods.** Scholastic, 1999.

Curtis, Jamie Lee. **Today I Feel Silly and Other Moods That Make My Day**. HarperCollins, 1998.

Hausman, Bonnie. **A to Z: Do You Ever Feel Like Me?** Dutton's Children's Books, 1999.

Glad Monster, Sad Monster: A Book About Feelings

Book Summary

This book is full of monsters of different colors. Each monster describes events that make him or her feel certain emotions. A foldout mask of each monster is included so that children can try on the mask and express their own emotions.

Lesson

1. Read the title of the book and ask students about the words "glad" and "sad."

2. Discuss feelings and emotions. Explain characterization to the students.

3. Read about the yellow monster and talk about why opening birthday presents, playing ball, eating ice cream and dancing with friends would make a person glad.

4. Choose one student to wear the yellow monster mask from the book and describe what makes him or her glad.

5. Continue reading the story, allowing different students to wear each monster mask and describe their feelings.

Additional Activity

Have students make their own feelings masks using a paper plate, construction paper, markers, scissors and glue.

Multiple Intelligences Addressed

Verbal/Linguistic Intelligence; Visual/Spatial Intelligence; Interpersonal Intelligence; Intrapersonal Intelligence; Body/Kinesthetic Intelligence; Logical/Mathematical Intelligence

On Monday When It Rained

Book Summary

Photographs and text describe the emotions a young boy feels each day of the week.

Lesson

1. Show the students the cover of *On Monday When It Rained*. Ask them how they think the little boy on the cover of the book is feeling.

2. Explain that this is a book about feelings. Explain characterization to the students.

3. Read the first page to the students. Have them use the words on the page to predict what the character might be feeling. Turn the page to discover the feeling word and the photograph that illustrates that feeling.

4. Continue reading the book in the same manner.

Additional Activity

Have students write a scenario about a feeling that they have had. Use a Polaroid or digital camera to take a picture of the student illustrating that feeling. Compile the students' texts, emotions and photographs into a class book patterned after *On Monday When It Rained*.

Multiple Intelligences Addressed

Verbal/Linguistic Intelligence; Visual/Spatial Intelligence; Intrapersonal Intelligence; Body/Kinesthetic Intelligence

How Are You Peeling? Foods with Moods

Book Summary

Fruits and vegetables are used to display a wide range of emotions from gentle to shy to secure.

Lesson

1. Read *How Are You Peeling? Foods with Moods* to the students.

2. Discuss characterization and the variety of feelings that students experience.

3. Brainstorm all of the feelings that the students can think of.

4. Ask each student to bring in a raw fruit or vegetable. Have them use a marker to illustrate a feeling on their fruit or vegetable. Then fold a piece of paper lengthwise and write a sentence describing their feeling.

5. Display the fruit or vegetable and their feeling on a table.

Multiple Intelligences Addressed

Verbal/Linguistic Intelligence; Visual/Spatial Intelligence; Interpersonal Intelligence; Intrapersonal Intelligence; Body/Kinesthetic Intelligence

Today I Feel Silly and Other Moods That Make My Day

Book Summary

A child describes her emotions, which range from silly to angry to joyful. She explains the reasons for each of her feelings and determines that each day brings different emotions, but each different feeling is acceptable.

Lesson

1. Explain characterization to the students.

2. Read the first page of *Today I Feel Silly and Other Moods That Make My Day* to the students. Determine that the character feels "silly." Ask the students for reasons why the character feels silly.

3. After each emotion, discuss the reason for the feeling.

4. Ask the students to draw a picture of how they are feeling today. Have them write a short paragraph at the bottom of the page about why they are feeling that way.

5. Ask the students to share their feelings with the class.

Multiple Intelligences Addressed

Verbal/Linguistic Intelligence; Visual/Spatial Intelligence; Interpersonal Intelligence; Intrapersonal Intelligence; Body/Kinesthetic Intelligence

A to Z: Do You Ever Feel Like Me?

Book Summary

A to Z: Do You Ever Feel Like Me? is an alphabet picture book that also has a riddle for each letter of the alphabet. The answer to each riddle is a feeling or emotion word. Photographs of children are additional clues to the answers.

Lesson

1. Prepare 26 9″ x 12″ posters. Each poster should have one two-inch letter in the top left corner. Give each student a poster.

2. Set a timer for 30 seconds and have the students write all of the feeling and emotion words they can think of that begin with their letter.

3. At the end of 30 seconds, pass each poster to another student and set the timer again. Continue until all 26 posters have several words, then hang the posters in alphabetical order.

4. Show students the cover of *A to Z: Do You Ever Feel Like Me?* Explain characterization to the students.

5. Read one riddle at a time and try to guess the answer. If the feeling or emotion word is not one of the words on the posters, have a student add the word.

   Example: From *A to Z: Do You Ever Feel Like Me?*:

   "I'm going to my grandparents.
   My clothes look snappy,
   My eyes are twinkling
   I feel so (h)." *The answer is happy.*

Additional Activity

Have students write their own feeling and emotion riddles. They can either illustrate their riddle or take photographs depicting their riddle.

Multiple Intelligences Addressed

Verbal/Linguistic Intelligence; Visual/Spatial Intelligence; Intrapersonal Intelligence; Body/Kinesthetic Intelligence

Words, Words, Words

Titles for Teaching Word Study

Individual words are the building blocks of reading. Word study is when students infer word meaning from context clues. Some ways to pick up context clues include: looking at the illustrations, reading the sentences before and after the unknown word and looking to see if the unknown word is followed by a comma and then a definition.

The more successful a student is at reading, the larger his or her vocabulary will be. The larger a student's vocabulary, the easier it is for him or her to infer word meaning. Two primary activities contribute to increasing a student's vocabulary. One is wide reading—listening to stories read aloud and reading on their own. The other is word play or experiencing the enjoyment of words.

Some successful ways to play with words are by playing games such as Hangman or Scrabble, creating unusual words and having teachers or adults point out new words as they come across them when reading aloud.

Books Used in This Chapter

Scieszka, Jon. ***Baloney (Henry P.)***. Viking, 2001.

Walton, Rick. ***Once There Was a Bull ... (Frog)***. Putnam Publishing Group, 1998.

Frasier, Debra. ***Miss Alaineus: A Vocabulary Disaster***. Harcourt, 2000.

Falwell, Cathryn. ***Word Wizard***. Clarion Books, 1998.

Clements, Andrew. ***Double Trouble in Walla Walla***. Millbrook Press, 1997.

Baloney (Henry P.)

Book Summary

When Henry's teacher asks him why he is late for school, he makes up a fantastic tall tale using at least 20 different Earth languages.

Lesson

1. Ask the students if they have ever been late to school. Brainstorm all of the excuses they can think of for being late. For example, forgetting to set the alarm clock.

2. Make a transparency of the word list on page 58. Ask students if they know the meaning of any of the words. Discuss what they think the words might mean.

3. Leave the transparency out and read *Baloney (Henry P.)* to the students.

4. Have the students use context clues—the pictures and words around the unknown word—to determine the meaning of the word. Write the predicted meaning next to each word on the transparency.

5. Discuss how the students came up with the meaning of each word. What context clues did they use to determine the meaning?

6. At the back of the book a decoder tells the meanings of the unknown words. Compare the true meanings with the students' predicted meanings. Discuss the different languages.

Multiple Intelligences Addressed

Verbal/Linguistic Intelligence; Visual/Spatial Intelligence; Interpersonal Intelligence

Baloney Words

Read *Baloney (Henry P.)*, then write the predicted meaning next to each word on the chart.

Unknown Word	Predicted Meaning
zimulis	
deski	
torakku	
szkola	
razzo	
pordo	
buttuna	
astrosus	
piksas	
giadrams	
cucalations	
kuningas	
blassa	
twrf	
sighing flosser	
fracasse	
uyarak	
zerplatzen	
speelplaats	
aamu	

Once There Was a Bull ... (Frog)

Book Summary

When a bullfrog from the Old West loses his hop, the reader must turn each page to see what compound word will be created and what will happen next in this lively tale.

Lesson

1. Read *Once There Was a Bull ... (Frog)* to the students. Pause each time you come to a bold-faced word in the text. In order to make sense of the plot, the bold-faced word from one page must be combined with the bold-faced word on the following page to create a compound word. The illustrations also provide clues to what the word will be.

2. As you read, students will begin to predict what the second part of the compound will be from the clues in the illustrations.

3. When you finish the story, make a list of all of the compound words in the text on a transparency or on chart paper. Discuss what each compound word means.

Additional Activity

Have each student fold a sheet of heavy paper in half lengthwise. On one side of the "tent," the student should illustrate the first half of a compound word. On the other side of the tent, the student should illustrate the second half of the compound word. On the inside of the tent, the student should write the compound word. For example, a picture of a foot might be on one side of the tent and a picture of a ball on the other. Inside the tent would say "football." Display the tents so the class can guess the compound words from the picture clues.

Multiple Intelligences Addressed

Verbal/Linguistic Intelligence; Visual/Spatial Intelligence; Interpersonal Intelligence

Miss Alaineus: A Vocabulary Disaster

Book Summary

Sage is home sick the day her teacher gives out the week's vocabulary list. When she returns, she gives the wrong definition in the Definition Bee. She thinks the word "miscellaneous" is "Miss Alaineus." Sage is embarrassed because her classmates find her definition hilarious. But with her mom's help, Sage uses her embarrassing mistake to create the winning entry for the class vocabulary parade.

Lesson

1. Read *Miss Alaineus: A Vocabulary Disaster* to the students.

2. Explain to the students that they can infer word meaning from context clues.

3. Hold a Vocabulary Bee. Use a list of vocabulary words that the students are studying. When a student is given a word, he or she must give a definition in his or her own words. If the definition is correct, the student goes to the back of the line and waits for the next word. If the definition is incorrect, the student must look up the word in the dictionary and give the correct definition.

Additional Activities

Have a vocabulary parade. Each student must sign up for a vocabulary word. The students make costumes that are creative interpretations of the word. Use the parade rules from "Sage's Vocabulary Parade Scrapbook" at the back of *Miss Alaineus: A Vocabulary Disaster*.

Have students make a vocabulary scrapbook. Each student must choose a vocabulary word and draw a creative interpretation of it. Compile the pages into a book.

Have students use the dictionary to write 26 sentences. The first sentence should contain three "A" words, the second three "B" words and so on through the alphabet. See "Extra! Extra! Extra Credit for Mrs. Page's Fifth-Grade Students!" in *Miss Alaineus: A Vocabulary Disaster*.

Multiple Intelligences Addressed

Verbal/Linguistic Intelligence; Visual/Spatial Intelligence; Logical/Mathematical Intelligence; Interpersonal Intelligence; Body/Kinesthetic Intelligence

Word Wizard

Book Summary

In *Word Wizard*, Anna uses her magical spoon to make new words by changing letters around. She uses her magical "word power" to help a lost little boy.

Lesson

1. Read *Word Wizard* to the students. Point out how Anna accomplishes the "magical" feat of rearranging the letters in a word to create new words. Use magnetic or cutout letters to show how Anna rearranged the letters.

2. Divide students into groups of two or three. Give each group a set of letters and have them make as many words as possible. Each group should make a list of their words on a sheet of paper.

3. After 5–10 minutes, ask the students to write a story using their words. Before the end of class, each group should have a chance to tell their story.

Multiple Intelligences Addressed

Verbal/Linguistic Intelligence; Visual/Spatial Intelligence; Interpersonal Intelligence; Logical/Mathematical Intelligence; Body/Kinesthetic Intelligence

Double Trouble in Walla Walla

Book Summary

It's an ordinary day in Walla Walla until Lulu is caught up in a word warp of chitter-chatter. This strange illness infects her teacher, the school nurse and the principal.

Lesson

1. Read the first four pages of *Double Trouble in Walla Walla* to the students. Use a transparency or chart paper to list all of the double words that have appeared so far. For example: Walla Walla, Lulu, nit-wit, higgledy-piggledy, tip-top, etc.

2. Ask the students to try to remember as many double words as possible. Finish reading the story.

3. Add all of the double words that the students remember to the list. See if there are any double words they can think of that are not in the book.

4. Make a bulletin board with the title "Double Trouble Words." Leave a supply of brightly colored markers and index cards beside the bulletin board.

5. Ask the students to add to the bulletin board during the next few days. They can put up any double words that they hear or find in the dictionary.

Multiple Intelligences Addressed

Verbal/Linguistic Intelligence; Visual/Spatial Intelligence; Interpersonal Intelligence; Intrapersonal Intelligence; Body/Kinesthetic Intelligence

Same Sorts of Sounds

Titles for Teaching Alliteration

Alliteration is when two or more words in a phrase have the same initial sound. Authors often use alliteration for emphasis and to make their writing more fun to read. When browsing through the books in a library, it is amazing to note how often titles contain alliteration. Some examples are:

- *Tikki Tikki Tembo* by Arlene Mosel
- *Arthur's April Fool* by Marc Brown
- *Pete's a Pizza* by William Steig

As an introduction, have students search the library shelves for more examples. Students might also like to try making their names alliterative. They might try:

- Marvelous Mandy
- Kind Kelly
- Generous Jeremy (Note that the initial sound is the same even though the beginning letters are not.)

Books Used in This Chapter

Edwards, Pamela Duncan. *Some Smug Slug*. HarperCollins, 1996.

Miranda, Anne. *Alphabet Fiesta*. Turtle Books, 2001.

Sendak, Maurice. *Alligators All Around: An Alphabet*. HarperCollins, 1990.

Bayer, Jane. *A My Name is Alice*. Dial Books for Young Readers, 1987.

Gerstein, Mordicai. *The Absolutely Awful Alphabet*. Harcourt, 2001.

Some Smug Slug

Book Summary

When a smug slug ignores the warnings of a sparrow, spider, swallowtail and other "S" animals, he comes to an unfortunate end. Throughout the book, the author incorporates alliteration with the letter "S" and the illustrator contributes to the fun by hiding an "S" shape in each picture.

Lesson

1. Read *Some Smug Slug* to the students.

2. Ask the students if they noticed anything unusual about the words in the story. When the students tell you that many of the words began with the letter "S," discuss alliteration.

3. Have the students try to remember as many of the "S" words as possible. Write them on a transparency or on chart paper.

4. Read the book again and have a student check off each word as soon as it appears in the story. Add any words that were not on the list.

5. For fun, search for the hidden "S" shape in each picture.

Additional Activity

Ask students to write about an animal using alliteration like in *Some Smug Slug*. They can research the animal if they need to. If they like, they can also illustrate their story and hide the shape of the letter in their illustration.

Multiple Intelligences Addressed

Verbal/Linguistic Intelligence; Visual/Spatial Intelligence; Interpersonal Intelligence; Musical/Rhythmic Intelligence; Naturalistic Intelligence

Alphabet Fiesta

Book Summary

Zelda Zebra's mother secretly invites all of Zelda's friends to a surprise birthday party. As the alphabet parade of animals make their way to the zoo for the fiesta, students experience alliteration and fun in both English and Spanish.

Lesson

1. Show the students the illustrations in *Alphabet Fiesta* and explain that they were illustrated by students in Spain.

2. Read the introduction to the story where Zelda Zebra's mother invites Armando Armadillo to Zelda's birthday party.

3. Point out how many of the words on this page begin with the letter "A." Explain that each page will be about a different animal that has been invited to the party.

4. If possible, have someone read the Spanish translation of the "A" page and look for "A" words in Spanish.

5. Use a chart containing all of the letters of the alphabet and ask students to predict which animals they think will be invited to the party.

6. Read the rest of *Alphabet Fiesta* and discuss which predictions were correct.

Multiple Intelligences Addressed

Verbal/Linguistic Intelligence; Visual/Spatial Intelligence; Interpersonal Intelligence

Alligators All Around: An Alphabet

Book Summary

This delightful ABC book has an alligator family navigate through the alphabet with alliteration on each and every page.

Lesson

1. Read *Alligators All Around: An Alphabet* to the students.

2. Discuss alliteration. Have the students tell you which words on each page are alliterative.

3. Explain how the author/illustrator, Maurice Sendak, took the alliteration in the title, *Alligators All Around,* and made the alligators the main characters in a story where each letter of the alphabet is the basis of an alliterative phrase that adds to the story's plot.

4. Have the students write an alliterative alphabet book using the book as a pattern. Example:

    A   amazing anteaters
    B   buying bananas
    C   create creatures
    D   drawing dinosaurs, etc.

Multiple Intelligences Addressed

Verbal/Linguistic Intelligence; Musical/Rhythmic Intelligence; Naturalistic Intelligence

A My Name is Alice

Book Summary

A My Name is Alice is an adaptation of a ball-bouncing game. In the rhyme, the alphabet becomes a playground for children's imaginations. Each letter features a husband and wife team whose names begin with the same letter of the alphabet. They come from a country beginning with that same letter and sell items beginning with that same letter.

Lesson

1. Begin reading *A My Name is Alice* to the students, using a rhythmic reading voice.

2. After reading through three or four letters of the alphabet, point out that the important parts of each rhyme begin with the same letter of the alphabet.

3. Explain alliteration to the students.

4. Continue reading the book, asking the students to predict what kind of animal is being described. *Note: The animals are given at the bottom of the page and also begin with the designated letter of the alphabet. Less familiar animals are explained in the back.*

5. Assign each student a letter of the alphabet. They should use that letter to come up with a page for the class alphabet book. Have them follow the example given below.

   ___ my name is _____ and my friend's name is _____.
   We come from _____ and we sell _____.
   _____ is a _____.
   _____ is a _____.

Multiple Intelligences Addressed

Verbal/Linguistic Intelligence; Visual/Spatial Intelligence; Musical/Rhythmic Intelligence; Body/Kinesthetic Intelligence

The Absolutely Awful Alphabet

Book Summary

Mean and monstrous letters, from A (an awfully arrogant amphibian) to Z (a zig-zagging zoo-logical zany), inhabit the pages of this alliterative alphabet book.

Lesson

1. Discuss alliteration with the students.

2. Have students use their first name and an adjective that starts with the same letter to describe themselves. For example, Laughing Lucas or Singing Sarah. Remind students that their description should be positive rather than negative.

3. Read *The Absolutely Awful Alphabet* to the students. Point out how a monster is incorporated into each letter of the alphabet.

4. Put the letters of the alphabet into a grab bag. Have each student pick one letter. Make sure all 26 letters of the alphabet are chosen.

5. Have the students draw a monster using their letter as the base of the monster.

6. Then have the students write an alliterative sentence about their illustration. As many words as possible should begin with the student's letter. Students should use the following pattern:

   _____ (letter) is a/an _____ (adjective), _____ (adjective), _____ (noun) _____ (verb) _____ (phrase).

7. Compile the pages into a class book and let each student autograph the back cover.

Multiple Intelligences Addressed

Verbal/Linguistic Intelligence; Visual/Spatial Intelligence; Interpersonal Intelligence

Crash! Bang! Boom!

Titles for Teaching Onomatopoeia

Onomatopoeia is the naming of a thing or action by a vocal imitation of the sound associated with it. In other words, onomatopoeia words sound like their meanings. For example, *crash, bang* and *boom* are onomatopoeia words.

Students are fascinated by the word "onomatopoeia." It is such an unusual word that students delight in knowing its meaning and being able to pronounce it.

A good introduction to the meaning of onomatopoeia is to bring items such as bells, whistles, pots and pans, etc. to the classroom or media center. Use these items to make sounds. Then have students make up the onomatopoeia words for the sounds that the objects create.

Books Used in This Chapter

Cronin, Doreen. **Click, Clack, Moo: Cows That Type**. Simon & Schuster, 2000.

Gray, Libba Moore. **When Uncle Took the Fiddle**. Orchard Books, 1999.

Janowitz, Tama. **Hear That?** SeaStar Books, 2001.

Rylant, Cynthia. **Night in the Country**. Simon & Schuster, 1991.

Showers, Paul. **The Listening Walk**. HarperCollins, 1991.

Click, Clack, Moo: Cows That Type

Book Summary

Farmer Brown has a problem. His cows like to type. Soon, the cows and the chickens begin to make demands of Farmer Brown, but when he refuses to go along with their requests for electric blankets, they go on strike.

Lesson

Note: If possible, bring in an old typewriter for the students to see. Many of them may have never seen a typewriter and might not understand the sounds it makes.

1. Read *Click, Clack, Moo: Cows That Type* to the students.

2. Discuss onomatopoeia. Have the students tell you which words from the story are onomatopoeia.

3. Make transparencies of the text of the book. Highlight the onomatopoeia words or write them in a bright color.

4. Divide the students into the groups listed below. Read the book again, pausing at the onomatopoeia words so that the appropriate group can perform their sounds.

    Group 1: "click" sound
    Group 2: "clack" sound
    Group 3: "moo" sound
    Group 4: "clickety" sound
    Group 5: "quack" sound

Additional Activity

Read (or have a student read) *Click, Clack, Moo: Cows That Type* using onomatopoeia words provided by the class.

Multiple Intelligences Addressed

Verbal/Linguistic Intelligence; Visual/Spatial Intelligence; Interpersonal Intelligence; Body/Kinesthetic Intelligence; Musical/Rhythmic Intelligence

When Uncle Took the Fiddle

Book Summary

On a day when the entire family is too tired to do anything, Uncle picks up his fiddle and begins playing. Sleepy family members pick up their instruments and join in for a rollicking good time.

Lesson

1. Show the students the illustrations in *When Uncle Took the Fiddle.* Discuss what they think happens in the story.

2. Brainstorm a list of the musical instruments that are shown in the illustrations. Write them on a transparency or on chart paper. Be sure to include the homemade instruments like the jug and the washboard.

3. Ask the students to predict what sounds they think the instruments would make. Write the sound word beside the name of the instrument. Explain onomatopoeia.

4. Read *When Uncle Took the Fiddle* to the students, emphasizing the onomatopoeia words.

5. Compare the sound words on the students' list to those in the story.

Additional Activity

Divide the students into groups. Each group is a different musical instrument. Read the story and have the groups join in at the appropriate time. The students could also use real or home-made instruments.

Multiple Intelligences Addressed

Verbal/Linguistic Intelligence; Visual/Spatial Intelligence; Interpersonal Intelligence; Body/Kinesthetic Intelligence; Musical/Rhythmic Intelligence

Crash! Bang! Boom!: Titles for Teaching Onomatopoeia **71**

Hear That?

Book Summary

When a mother and son are home alone, they begin to hear strange noises. They make a game out of guessing what is making the unusual sounds.

Lesson

1. Discuss onomatopoeia with the students.

2. Explain that all of the following sounds are in *Hear That?* Divide the class into eight sound groups:

BUZZ! BUZZ! BUZZ!	TAP! TAP! TAP!
SQUEAK! SQUEAK! SQUEAK!	KNOCK! KNOCK! KNOCK!
SQUISH! SQUISH! SQUISH!	THUMP! THUMP! THUMP!
CLICK! CLICK! CLICK!	BOOM! BA-BOOM! BA-BOOM!

3. Each group should determine how they will make their sound. They may use their voices, hands, feet, etc.

4. Read *Hear That?* to the students, making sure they can see the pictures. Pause at the appropriate moments so the groups can perform their sounds.

5. On the page before the real reason for the sounds is revealed (Daddy), let all of the students make their sound at the same time.

Additional Activity

On the last page of the book, the characters hear a new sound. Ask the students to predict what they think that new sound will be.

Multiple Intelligences Addressed

Verbal/Linguistic Intelligence; Visual/Spatial Intelligence; Interpersonal Intelligence; Body/Kinesthetic Intelligence; Musical/Rhythmic Intelligence

Night in the Country

Book Summary

In *Night in the Country,* a child listens to all of the sounds that occur when the lights go out. The child hears the "reek reek reek" of the frogs, the "clank, clank" of the dog's chain and many other sounds that you hear only when you stop to listen.

Lesson

1. Read *Night in the Country* to the students.

2. Discuss the many sound words that were used in the book. Write the words on a transparency or on chart paper.

3. Explain onomatopoeia to the students.

4. Give the students a homework assignment. Provide each student with a brown paper sack. Ask them to bring in an object from home that makes a sound. (Examples: a bell, paper that makes a noise when crumpled, etc.) Have the students place the object in the sack and write the onomatopoeia word for the object's sound on the outside of the sack. During the next class, have the students try to guess what the object is from the onomatopoeia word on the outside of the sack.

Multiple Intelligences Addressed

Verbal/Linguistic Intelligence; Visual/Spatial Intelligence; Interpersonal Intelligence; Intrapersonal Intelligence

The Listening Walk

Book Summary

A little girl and her father take a quiet walk. Along the way, they identify the sounds they hear.

Lesson

1. Read *The Listening Walk* to the students.

2. Discuss the many sound words that were used in the book. Write the words on a transparency or on chart paper.

3. Explain onomatopoeia to the students.

4. Take the students on a listening walk. Have each student carry a journal to write the onomatopoeia words for all of the sounds that they hear. Stress the importance of silence on the listening walk so that everyone can hear the sounds.

5. After the listening walk, discuss the onomatopoeia words that the students created.

6. Have the students write sentences using their sounds, then illustrate the sentences. Compile the sentences and pictures into a book.

Multiple Intelligences Addressed

Verbal/Linguistic Intelligence; Visual/Spatial Intelligence; Body/Kinesthetic Intelligence; Intrapersonal Intelligence; Interpersonal Intelligence; Naturalistic Intelligence

Grouchy as a Bear

Titles for Teaching Similes

Authors often use comparisons to describe an object, action or feeling. A simile is a figure of speech in which one thing is compared to another using the word *like* or *as*. Students are often familiar with comparisons such as:

- "as grouchy as a bear"

- "as quick as a fox"

- "as hard as a rock"

When students learn that these are similes, they are excited about sharing more common similes that they have heard. One way that you can expand your students' knowledge of similes is to explain that authors often create unusual similes to make their writing more clear or interesting. An example is:

The teacher was proud of her students when they all passed their math test. *She was as proud as a new mother showing off her baby for the first time.*

Books Used in This Chapter

Schwartz, David M. ***If You Hopped Like a Frog***. Scholastic, 1999.

Wood, Audrey. ***Quick as a Cricket***. Child's Play International, 1996.

Lindbergh, Reeve. ***Grandfather's Lovesong***. Viking, 1995.

Leedahl, Shelley A. ***The Bone Talker***. Red Deer Press, 2000.

Modesitt, Jeanne. ***Sometimes I Feel Like a Mouse***. Scholastic, 1992.

If You Hopped Like a Frog

Book Summary

If You Hopped Like a Frog compares what humans could do if they had the characteristics of various animals. The book introduces children to similes and ratios, so it can also be used to integrate language arts and mathematics.

Lesson

1. Read the letter from the author in the front of the book.

2. Ask the students to imagine what it would be like to jump like a frog. Discuss their ideas.

3. Read the first few pages of the book, discussing what it would be to "hop like a frog," be "as strong as an ant," to "have the brain of a Brachiosaurus" and to "swallow like a snake."

4. Provide each student with an index card. Each card should have a simile from the book.
   If you ate like a shrew ...
   If you high-jumped like a flea ...
   If you flicked your tongue like a chameleon ...
   If you craned your neck like a crane ...
   If you had eagle eyes ...
   If you dined like a pelican ...
   If you scurried like a spider ...
   If you hugged like a bear ...

5. Have the students use their prediction skills to complete the comparison.

6. Explain that comparisons using the words *like* or *as* are called similes.

7. Finish reading *If You Hopped Like a Frog* to the students.

8. Discuss whether the students came up with any of the same comparisons that the author did.

Multiple Intelligences Addressed

Verbal/Linguistic Intelligence; Visual/Spatial Intelligence; Logical/Mathematical Intelligence; Interpersonal Intelligence; Intrapersonal Intelligence

Quick as a Cricket

Book Summary

The child in *Quick as a Cricket* compares himself with a variety of animals. Each description, such as "I'm as sad as a basset, I'm as happy as a lark," is a simile.

Lesson

1. Read *Quick as a Cricket* to the students.

2. Discuss similes.

3. Ask the students to brainstorm similes that describe various class members. For example, "Kelly is as fast as a cheetah" or "Jeremy is as cuddly as a teddy bear." Be sure to remind students that the similes should always be positive. This will prevent hurt feelings.

4. Ask the students to write six simile statements about themselves. For example, "I'm as smart as an encyclopedia." Once again, remind students that all similes should be positive rather than negative.

5. Photocopy the pattern on page 78 for each student. Have the students cut out their cubes. On each face of the cube, the students should write one simile statement and illustrate it. Fold the paper into a cube and glue it together.

6. Hang the simile cubes from the ceiling for display.

Multiple Intelligences Addressed

Verbal/Linguistic Intelligence; Visual/Spatial Intelligence; Body/Kinesthetic Intelligence; Interpersonal Intelligence

Simile Cubes

Cut out the pattern along the solid black lines. On each face of the cube, write one simile statement and illustrate it. Fold the paper along the dotted lines, so it forms a cube. Glue the tabs to the inside of the cube.

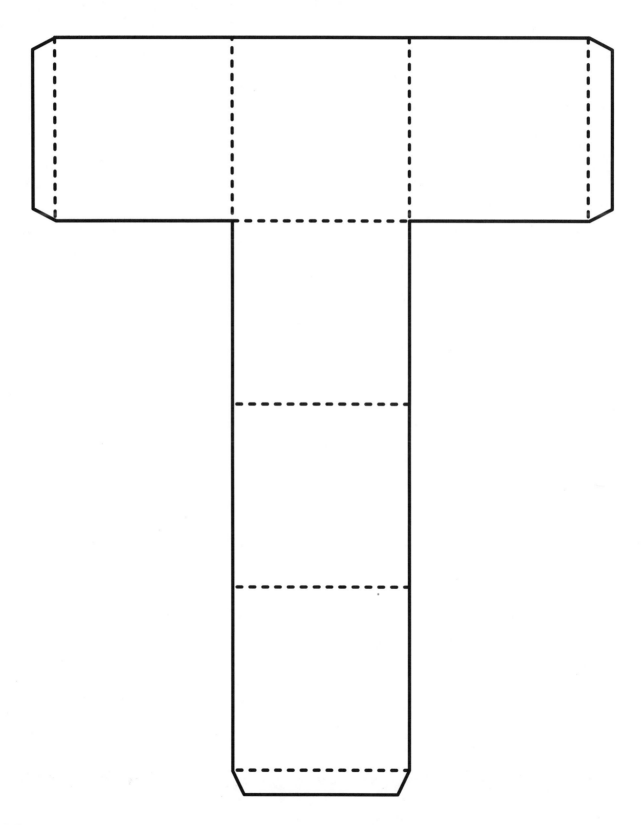

Grandfather's Lovesong

Book Summary

A grandfather and his grandchild wander through the beautiful seasons of the year. The grandfather uses similes to express how much he loves his grandson.

Lesson

1. Read *Grandfather's Lovesong* to the students.

2. Explain similes to the students. This book is filled with similes as the grandfather compares his love for his grandson with things that the child understands. Reread parts of the book and discuss the comparisons.

3. Provide each student with an 8½″ x 11″ piece of construction paper and instruct students to fold it into a greeting card.

4. Explain that the students are going to make a card for someone they love. It can be for anyone that the child is close to.

5. On the inside of the card the students should write a simile expressing how much they love that person. Use the similes in *Grandfather's Lovesong* as an example.

6. Have the students illustrate the front of the cards, sign them and deliver them.

Multiple Intelligences Addressed

Verbal/Linguistic Intelligence; Visual/Spatial Intelligence; Body/Kinesthetic Intelligence; Interpersonal Intelligence; Intrapersonal Intelligence

The Bone Talker

Book Summary

Grandmother Bones has grown old and "wound down like a clock." Everyone in the village is worried about her and wants to make her happy. But no one is able to until a small child discovers the secret to Grandmother Bones's happiness.

Lesson

1. Prepare enough 5" x 5" construction paper squares so that each child has 10–12 pieces of various colors. The paper squares will eventually form a quilt like one Grandmother Bones makes at the end of the story.

2. Discuss similes with the students. Tell them that this story is filled with similes. As they hear a simile, they should write it on one of their squares with a black marker.

3. Slowly read *The Bone Talker* to the students. Give them time to write down each simile. It might help if you write the similes on a transparency or on chart paper as you come to them in the story.

4. Have the students complete their squares. Put the quilt together on a wall as a remembrance of a great story.

Multiple Intelligences Addressed

Verbal/Linguistic Intelligence; Visual/Spatial Intelligence; Body/Kinesthetic Intelligence

Sometimes I Feel Like a Mouse

Book Summary

In *Sometimes I Feel Like a Mouse*, a child imagines becoming a variety of animals while experiencing different feelings: a howling wolf for sad, a soaring eagle for proud, a stomping elephant for bold, etc.

Lesson

1. Discuss similes. Explain that *Sometimes I Feel Like a Mouse* has a simile on every page.

2. Hold the book so the students can see the illustrations, but not the text.

3. Read all of the text on the first page, except for the word "shy." Tell the students that the "feeling word" in the simile is "shy."

4. Continue reading in this manner. Have the students guess each feeling word from the description given in the simile.

Additional Activity

Have the students think of similes that describe them. Use the similes in *Sometimes I Feel Like a Mouse* as examples. Ask students who wish to share their simile to recite it in front of the class, but leave out the feeling word. See if the class can determine the feeling that each student is describing.

Multiple Intelligences Addressed

Verbal/Linguistic Intelligence; Visual/Spatial Intelligence; Interpersonal Intelligence; Intrapersonal Intelligence